ON SUN SWALLOWING

by Dakota Warren

First Edition, 2021
Copyright © Dakota Warren
All rights reserved

www.dakotawarren.com

Published by Pure Nowhere
www.purenowhere.com
hello@purenowhere.com

ISBN: 978-0-6454066-0-3

Cover Image by Francesca McConnell
Cover Design by Abby Strangward and Kyla Rain

Printed and bound in Naarm/Melbourne, Australia, by E-Plot Printing

On Sun Swallowing was written on the stolen land of the Wurundjeri people of the Kulin Nation. We acknowledge them as the traditional owners of the land and pay our respects to their elders past, present and emerging. Sovereignty was never ceded.

Sell your soul

Sign here : ....

CONTENTS

i.

SEA-FOAM SICK
THE ART OF BONE CARVING
CLAY / TWO NIGHTS AND MAYBE THREE DAYS
FUNERAL SONG
A NOTE ON REVERENCE
PAS DE DEUX
ON GIRLHOOD
SLEEP PARALYSIS
A PATERNAL EXPOSÉ
HOME OF THE FERAL FOLK
THE ART OF RUNNING AWAY
3.01PM
RAMBLINGS OF A REALIST (the 6 stages of acceptance)
ENTROPY
MIRRORS ARE BEST KEPT HIDDEN

ii.

STINKING PSYCHOPOMP SUCCUBUS
CROSSROADS
FORGET-ME-NOT
6.33PM
INSOMNIAC'S LULLABY (after Inferno)
IT'S PURGATORY BUT IT'S LIVEABLE
LESSONS I LEARNED THE SUMMER OF SCRAPED KNEES
   AND CAFFEINE
I DATED AN ARCHITECT ONCE
RAW MATERIAL
LIGHTS, CAMERA, ACTION
GOD IS COCKTAIL ON A SATURDAY NIGHT
IMMORTALITY FOR ABSURDISTS
A COLLECTION OF THOUGHTS FROM FEBRUARY
HALF-SPRUNG
MONDAY FORGETS ABOUT THE DREAMERS

iii.

SUNDAY MORNING PSYCHOSIS
9.09PM
THE BLOOD ON HUMBERT'S HANDS
EXTRACT FROM A LOVE LETTER OR MURDER CONFESSION
SWITCHBLADE
SUMMER'S SALVATION
PHILOSOPHY BETWEEN COTTON SHEETS
THE SUN IS BOUND TO IMPLODE
ROT IN STAGES
LILITH
INTRUSIVE THOUGHTS
3.33AM
KLEOS
AN ODE TO THE AUSTRALIAN DIRT BENEATH MY FEET
ON SUN SWALLOWING

AUTHOR'S NOTE

Dearest reader,

Please know the contents contained within this book are nothing if not a safe space for all.

Sure, these words are mine, and sure, the ink is my blood, but you are the one who now holds these words between your hands. The exchange has been done, the ritual is complete. My words are now yours, and it is none of my business whether you swallow them whole or fuse them with your own blood so we can create something new, together. We are all artists here.

On Sun Swallowing is a collection of poetry, prose and journal extracts which endeavours to affirm the validity of the gloriously twisted enigma one is. Relish in the duality of being a hard-soft thing. Dismantle dichotomy and exist as yourself, deliciously undefinable.

Each entry subtly unfolds to comprise my own cryptic and obscure sense of self. I relish in my youth and femininity - all things soft, dreamy and delicate, but drenched in gasoline and set ablaze. You are cordially invited to wedge yourself between my words, regardless of your own expression of gender, philosophy, religion, and ever-changing identity.

Become both needle and thread and loop yourself around my intimacies with girlhood, godhood and the dark things that lurk between. Follow my hunt for resolution and be met with a lust for wickedness.

Remember: you are safe here.

I love you an impossible amount simply for holding this book between your hands.

Please take care of yourself whilst you indulge in my hedonistic mediocrities and please remember I am perhaps the most unreliable narrator of them all.

Love always,

Dakota Warren

CONTENT WARNING

This book explores my personal trials and tribulations with themes that may be of sensitivity, such as: mental illness/disorders, religious trauma, violence and substance usage.

i. *for Plath*

"I need a father, I need a mother, I need some older, wiser being to cry to. I talk to God, but the sky is empty, and Orion walks by and doesn't speak."

— Sylvia Plath, *The Unabridged Journals of Sylvia Plath*

SEA-FOAM SICK

We always thought the future would be
softer, kinder, maybe a little more erotic;
instead we suck the rot from our navels
swallow the sadism or spit it in Latin
and kiss each other with the same mouth.

And as Aphrodite was birthed
glorious and new and drenched
in the nectar of the sea
I shall crawl inside a clam and make
my father proud, emerging
glorious and new and drenched
in the pearlescence of
my doom.

Your rot is mine and
my rot is yours and
why does decay feel so soiled
when it promises to birth us
unferal -
softer, kinder, maybe a little more erotic
and new, brand new,
clean with that
new car scent.

Maybe that way
we can trick
our fathers
into wanting us.

THE ART OF BONE CARVING

I have washed my hands twelve times
today but I still have blood dried
under my fingernails from January.
My flesh is stained with what we did
and you called it art and I'll call it murder
but what matters most
is the space we earned
on the panel of impending
doom.

All that's important is we're in this
together, so tell me you love me but don't
try and kiss me because I don't need touch
to know truth.

Carve out my bones
like we carved out a heart
in the trunk of a sycamore tree,
and promise me
you can keep this secret forever.

CLAY / TWO NIGHTS AND MAYBE THREE DAYS

Do you remember when I hadn't slept
for two nights and maybe three days

and we were sat on the veranda out front,
cracked concrete and peeling paint, insect upon

insect seeking solace from the Australian sun?
Do you remember when I told you I was afraid

my skin was clay and if I sat for too long I might
set, harden, bake into a teacup or a ceramic

glazed bowl, painted blue with specks of grey
and, oh, my, is that a tear rolling down my face?

Do you remember when I held the vibrating body
of a dragonfly between my middle and forefinger,

this luminous symbol of a childhood passed posed
like a cigarette, us staring, it begging to escape,

and you breathed, stop it, you're hurting it, and I
couldn't hear you because I was clay, and I was

setting, and I was clay, and I was setting, a blue
and grey speckled teacup sat cross-legged

on the cracked concrete and peeling paint and
temporary insect asylum veranda out front?

FUNERAL SONG

i. We say he is at peace now because we cannot stand the thought of horror after death.

ii. I killed him. You killed him. I held the dagger and you plunged it into his chest and sometimes the sky leaks divinity and pretends it is rain. Ripened flesh rots fast, the way stone-fruit tends, and you can hold the plum gently between calloused hands but it will still bleed. We are murderers, liars, thieves, but our lives will be long, and they tell us not to cheat but we've never come second place.

iii. God died before we were born. Our grandparents felt the last of him, that's why they nail crosses above their beds and drape rosaries from their necks. There's no heaven anymore and they'll take that to their grave. He'll be stuck in limbo and we'll probably meet Him there and just because we're baptised doesn't mean we're owed salvation. The angels are homesick and they can't find their wings, and I think I met an angel in hospital, but we're sick, and they're dying, and there's a difference. There is a difference. We all have blood on our hands but we're all too clean for hell.

A NOTE ON REVERENCE

I suppose I believe in a God the way I believe in a father;
I only want it to be real when I'm afraid of the dark,
I only want it to be real when I'm afraid of dying.

Somebody once told me capitalising the G's in God was evidence of my Catholic upbringing because apparently the agnostics don't do that anymore, so I suppose by denouncing years of religious trauma (*think: middle-class private school compulsory prayers before recess and mandatory damnation after lunch*) I should probably abandon salvation or capital G's, but I'm a sucker for punctuation and old habits tend to die hard.

So I suppose what I'm trying to say is, dear reader, when I summon God or Lucifer or the angels of the midnight sun, please know that it is merely my rotten way of coping turned to

a questionable
kind of art.

PAS DE DEUX

    I lost everything I love, but
    I've started dancing again.

    My bones still pop and suck like quicksand,
    my pirouettes still veer
to the left
    and I still don't think before I speak, but
    my hair is strawberry blonde now
    and I have stopped telling lies.
    I think you'd be proud of me for that.

    My ballet teachers taught me
even falling should be graceful.

ON GIRLHOOD

i. I am fifteen years old and I hold the stars within my bambi eyes and long golden locks licking and curling at my hips like flames. I take my first pay-cheque earned from scanning bread and milk after school for two days a week to the dingy chemist down the road and stuff my fists with effervescent vitamin B and appetite suppressing gum. I know it's a placebo, but that won't stop me. It won't stop any of us. The hard-faced lady at the counter scans me from head to toe and narrows her eyelids, heavy and hooded with soft wrinkles. What is she looking for? An indication of age, of innocence, of extra weight on my chest? With pursed lips she takes my shiny new bank card between her thumb and forefinger stained yellow from tobacco. I passed her test. Was it the sparkle in my eyes? The roundness in my cheeks? You don't need that, honey. You're just a girl. Her voice is softer than her face. I pick at the thick skin at the edges of my nails and dare not lock eyes with the hard-soft thing telling me what I am not. You're just a girl. Her words reverberate in my skull like a choir in an empty church as I trudge to the bus stop. You're just a girl, you're just a girl, you're just a girl.

ii. The irony of Frankenstein dreaming of gutting his creation with the blade of a rifle is the same irony that lays within the ribcage of the girl who kisses boys to pass the time and kisses girls to curve the righteousness. Am I the creator or the destroyer, the blade or the belly? Secrets are in the bones that make up our very spines and every day is our last. Are you tired? Are you bored? You're just a girl. Girlhood is barefoot hot summer nights sticky-sweet with salted sweat, bruised shins and bony ankles and chipped cherry-red nail polish, watching sunsets from the school-bus and sealing love letters addressed to the science teacher with a half-dried glue-stick before sliding it under his office door. Girls shouldn't have hair falling out in clumps and dried blood under their fingernails and blackened knees from kneeling on the cold bathroom tiles like a gargoyle on a weathered rooftop, begging the scales for salvation. Begging isn't pretty and pretty is all we have.

We're just girls, after all.

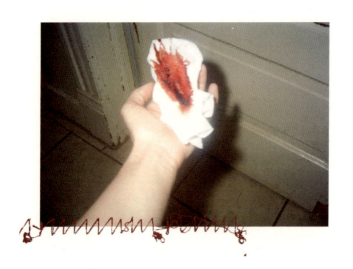

SLEEP PARALYSIS

9.22 PM

I grow horns
something biblical,
rather unspectacular

10.44 PM

The thirst for annihilation
consumes shards
of broken stars

11.11 PM

We wish
for hedonistic dissolution
(or love)

2.31 AM

I can taste the salvation
the church had promised me
it is like the barrel of a gun
between my front teeth

4.54 AM

A cherubim holds my hand
be not afraid,
little one
I do not speak Enochian

6.16 AM

Le soleil se lève
alas,
my shadow is asleep.

A PATERNAL EXPOSÉ

Dearest Father,
I hope this finds you well.
Today I stained 'The Book of Lies' with a bleeding
pomegranate, flesh somewhere between ripe and rotting.
Tonight I am a bleeding pomegranate, flesh somewhere
between ripe and rotting. It is a strange thing to
hold a body so young but a heart so ancient. Does
~~yours~~- your chest feel like rusted pipes too? Aleister
Crowley was a little insane but he was a poet and all
poets are a little unwell, aren't we? I think you
influenced him a lot more than he'd like to admit. I
think you influence me more than I'd like to admit, too.
My mother is so full of love and I am so full of darkness
and I could only have inherited that from you. Is the
Inferno as ~~hota-~~ hot as Dante promised? Can I come and
stay for a while? I'm getting tired of all the goodness
in the world. I tried to summon you again, but I think
you were too busy condemning. Is it possible to miss
somebody you've never met? I miss you.
I hope to hear from you soon.

Love always,
The Devil's Daughter.

"Love death therefore, and long eagerly for it.
 Die daily."
                -Aleister Crowley, The Book of Lies

HOME OF THE FERAL FOLK

Here from the feral folk comes a daughter of dirt,
seraphim of barefoot ballet -
gum nuts and scraped knees sing to little lambs
while the ravens await their stoic decay.

We hide behind haystacks with a rifle of rust;
farmers and monsters, this is our home -
eyes in the bushes, where demons roam
waiting for foxes and teenage boys.

There's an angel in the bushland behind
the local church and with bloodied teeth
it smiles and mouths *run or you'll get hurt*.
No man's land, population ninety-three -

Child, this small town will swallow you whole
if you don't kiss your mother and leave.

THE ART OF RUNNING AWAY

Winter scampers past
with heavy feet,
balmy cul-de-sac mornings
thick with black fog,
tucked beneath

honeyed street-lamps and naked
trees - these are the tender moments
we lose ourselves.

And sure, spring might have sprung
and sure, the walk home isn't long
and sure, if you say this is where you belong

we have no reason not to
believe you. So go on,
they won't wait for too long-

hitch up your skirt on the highway of
bones and show them what makes you

different.

3.01PM

A SWEET DAY: NO LONGER HOLLOW BUT NOT QUITE WHOLE, SO THERE'S ROOM FOR WANTING. CATEGORISED BOOKS IN STACKS OF DECEIT, FORAGED LAVENDER FROM THE CATHOLIC SCHOOL ON THE HILL, ROLLER-SKATED ON THE KITCHEN TILES TO SOFT JAZZ, LAID FACE-UP IN THE SUN TILL I COULD COUNT ELEVEN NEW FRECKLES, NO LESS, NO MORE. I'M BEGINNING TO ADORE THE MONSTER IN THE MEDICINE CABINET MIRROR.

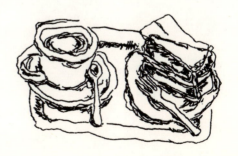

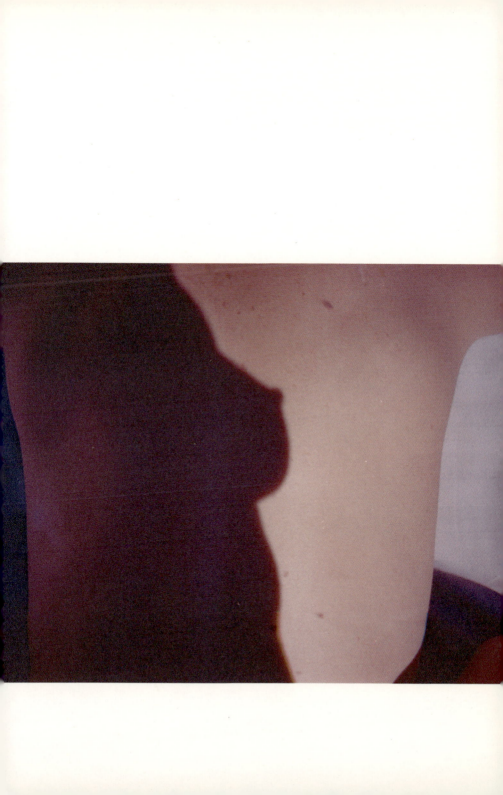

RAMBLINGS OF A REALIST
(OR THE 6 STAGES OF ACCEPTANCE)

i) The stomach of philosophy is a bottomless pit and she is hungry, she is hungry, she is hungry.

ii) We're all searching for something. Don't think you're unique for looking in the wrong places.

iii) The earth is sick, less dying than dead, and extinction is now more promise than threat but we've already tasted the apocalypse.

iv) The schools won't teach you about the void, how it is thicker than milk but softer than bathroom tiles.

v) Some people are afraid that the world is ending. The rest of us are lying.

vi) So, how good are you at pretending? Are you lost, are you bored, or just familiar with the ending?

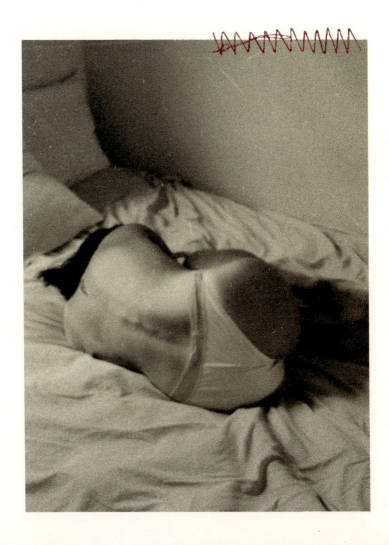

ENTROPY

I obsess over the absurd   and convince myself
     I can have   everything
     if I so much as

ask.

I am an angel who lies   to God
spends her days on the border of hell,
seducing the demons with
        piano fingers
        and
        big
            wet
              brown
                  eyes.

I don't expect   forgiveness
    and I'll never ask   for understanding
but when the days get warmer

    I wonder
    how it feels to be

clean.

I am the spawn of infidelity, the pretty blonde kind, the kind that makes headlines for being new. I am fuck eyes and toothy grins and the one who pirouettes on your grave. I am a lovesick wet dream, a saviour's hopeless thing. I am callous and I am prolific. I am birth and I am death. I am entropy.

                I am new, new, new.

MIRRORS ARE BEST KEPT HIDDEN

Pay homage to Aphrodite
when you kiss the bathroom floor -
moulded tiles against bare flesh
begging for something more (or less)

When did you start hating yourself?
When did you notice you were so far gone
gap-toothed and fawn-eyed and ground up teeth
sicker than you might have let on.
Dig a hole, go down the hole -
mirrors are best kept hidden.

You think of your mother when she was a girl,
was the world too big for her too? I profess:
I haven't slept for (I guess) four days now, so
excuse me if I'm not making much sense.

Mirrors are best kept hidden.

ii. *for Kafka*

"Forget everything. Open the windows. Clear the room. The wind blows through it. You see only its emptiness, you search in every corner and don't find yourself."

— Franz Kafka, *Diaries 1910-1923*

STINKING PSYCHOPOMP SUCCUBUS

Sticky sweet with
bonafide magic, fingertips laced / with
the kind of alchemy you recall from a past life / or
maybe a dream. I am my own magnum opus, / a myriad of
hedonism and stomach bile and spilled red wine / on piano keys.
You, hollow victories and scraped knees / and the lucky number
three, I loved you. I loved you / for two days and maybe three
nights, a fraction of a year / and you loved me for, I postulate,
the duration of winter / or something near. I still think about
it, you know / the wolfish love of the unholy gods, eating
ambrosia / with our hands in place of silver, heretic
at our very core / stinking psychopomp
succubus and her sidekick. / But don't
you see, boredom begs to be
broken / and the truth is
you were my neo-
noir love
affair.

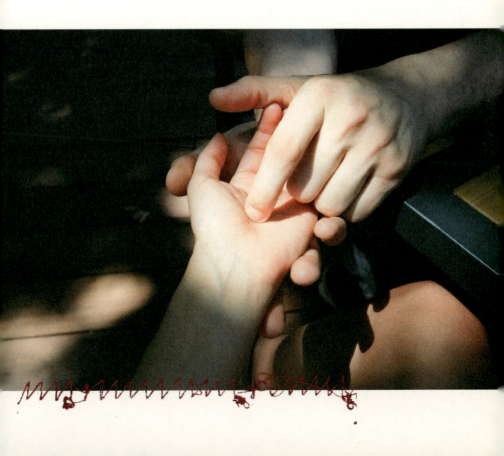

CROSSROADS

I built my bed at the crossroads - a place
where the heart of suburbia adorned with

jewels so regal and backstreets so meek
traverses the callous and unforgiving gaze

of a glass-house city stretched impossibly
tall to spy over fields of faith and lakes of lies

on girls like us to make sure we can't
see ourselves for who we truly are, or worse:

escape.

FORGET ME NOT

My seed was planted in a bed
of generational lies
and that's nothing against my mother.

It doesn't matter where I was planted.
Hell, it doesn't matter where I bloomed.

It matters where the children pluck me
from my waist and pull at my petals till
I tell them they're loved back.

6.33 PM

I'M THINKING OF PHASES
AND HOW I FILL

    SPACES

AND THE PLACES
I WANT TO DANCE IN.

INSOMNIAC'S LULLABY (after Inferno)

It is 3.13am and in milk-tooth slices
the moon pokes through blinds
and dapples my teenage bedroom alabaster
white, cotton ichor of a godless sky
planting silk-soft kisses on
half-chewed fingertips -

and if this is what they mean
by purgatory, please
tell my mum

I'm alright.

45

~~am tires~~
plague me with nostalgia.

IT'S PURGATORY
IT'S PURGATORY
IT'S PURGATORY
IT'S PURGATORY
IT'S PURGATORY
IT'S PURGATORY
IT'S PURGATORY
IT'S PURGATORY
IT'S PURGATORY

~~if fallo out in tiempo before it can work.~~

~~I would prefer if you didn't~~
~~for if you didn't read my coe~~

BUT IT'S LIVEABLE
BUT IT'S LIVEABLE
BUT IT'S LIVEABLE
BUT IT'S LIVEABLE
BUT IT'S LIVEABLE
BUT IT'S LIVEABLE
BUT IT'S LIVEABLE
BUT IT'S LIVEABLE
BUT IT'S LIVEABLE

~~I would prefer if you didn't rea~~

LESSONS I LEARNED IN THE SUMMER OF SCRAPED KNEES AND CAFFEINE

I learned to be alone, I learned to be ~~lovely~~ lonely,
and I learned of the space in between.

✴ I learned writing in cursive induces something morbid.

I learned that I am small, very mortal,
and incomprehensibly defenceless.

I learned that falling asleep in dresses and pearls
wakes me up beautiful.

I learned that I was lost (or rather, reminded).

I learned that lost is nice when you're not ready to be found.

I learned that memories cannot be made
when I lock my bedroom door.

✸ I learned how to love a girl gently and now I never want to leave.

I learned of the transition from hating your mother to pitying her.

I learned that the dogs guarding the gates of hell are the furthest thing from evil. They're only doing their job.

I learned that I should not have caffeine.
(I still consumed copious amounts of caffeine.)

I learned the Australian sun is angry and out for blood.

I learned I am the villain the civilians secretly root for because they are tired of all the goodness.

I learned to stop running from myself.

I DATED AN ARCHITECT ONCE

and I may not know of pilasters and plinths
and the buildings of Byzantine, but
I know to build upon rubble and ash
would be a waste of both effort and time.

Put the pen
        down, baby

you can't build a home
                here.

RAW MATERIAL

They tell me to write something from my heart, but
they do not know that I was born
with a hole, a gap, an empty crevice,
a labyrinth of blood and spit
and flesh and teeth, so instead
I must craft my magnum opus from this thing,
this chamber of bones, and launch it
into space in hope it will reach

some kind of heaven.

LIGHTS, CAMERA, ACTION

Between us we pass a bottle of wine-too-sweet and drink
from it with bee-stung lips, wiping the spill on our chins
with the backs of freckled wrists. We wear nothing but

bikini bottoms on the dying grass of our borrowed backyard
pretending we are safe from the Australian sun and her fury.
Tonight we will stuff tender reddened skin into our very best

frocks adorned with the finest silk and milk-maid sleeves and
only a fistful of rot, and pad barefoot on scalding roads more
melted tar than path. We will dance under street-lamps that

we mistake for the sun and kiss strangers in the dark corners
of hot nights and maybe we will fall in love and maybe
we will die. These nights are laced with something mean,

some kind of drug or just nicotine, to keep us small, skinny,
and dangerously lean, but it is only tucked beneath these
forbidden nights that we remember to exist is to perform

so we dance.

GOD IS A COCKTAIL ON A SATURDAY NIGHT

I drunkenly ask for a definition of God, exhaling the request
with cigarette smoke.

She replies:
God is a cocktail on a Saturday night.

He replies:
God is a whiskey sour telling me to do bad things.

She replies:
God was an exploding star.

He replies:
An exploding star that became a cocktail 4.5 billion years later.

I furrow my brows and finish my half-full vodka martini
in one long sip.

I reply:
Your God lies in my stomach and I think I'm going to throw up.

IMMORTALITY FOR ABSURDISTS

Pick a god and pray to it, child
crawl on all fours and beg for your raison d'être.

Prayers disguised as a sonnet
for the ones who wept -
the poets left faithless in crops stripped bare
who mourned the death of a season
the citrus tree in your childhood home
who mourned the loss of her lemons
the father with the daughter growing fangs
who mourned the loss of his little girl.

Bury me shallow, I'll be back -
we can't count the stars, but you can count
on my resurrection.

A COLLECTION OF THOUGHTS FROM FEBRUARY

Pink skies plague me with nostalgia.

~~I would prefer if you didn't read my co~~
I WOULD PREFER IF YOU DIDN'T READ MY BRAIN LIKE THAT.

The fool is innocent to himself and his dreams.

I am tired of selling my soul to impress strangers.

On colder days I really do believe I may be dying.

Will I still be a poet on the other side?
Will my body decompose before the afterlife?
I would like my flesh to rot to Claude Debussy, please, if I am allowed to request things post-mortem.

I am a ballerina who waltzes to rock music.

I am the universe confined in turmoil,
begging to be seen.

I cried at a cemetery, only strangers beneath the earth as company.

Latency is not something that can be taught, and even if it could,
I'm not a very good teacher.

PORCELAIN STATUES SHED TEARS OF BUTTERFLY MILK.

They are not crying from despair, nor loss, nor grief - merely confusion.

So am I.

I have been confused for one million years.

The moon taught me to ask questions and the sun showed me how to answer them.

God told me to start a cult and Satan dared me to start a revolution.

I clipped my wings so I could fit inside your arms, but your hold made me claustrophobic.

Some nights I think fear might just swallow me whole, but that's to be expected when you can hear death.

It sounds like a swarm of wasps inside your brain, each trying to tell you a different thing at once in a language you remember to forget.

~~*Your hair falls out in clumps before it can grow back.*~~ Your hair falls out in clumps before it grows back.

I tried to make it fall out again, but it can only happen once.

DON'T PULL AT IT, YOU'LL ONLY MAKE IT WORSE.

It's more fun when it's a secret,

anyway.

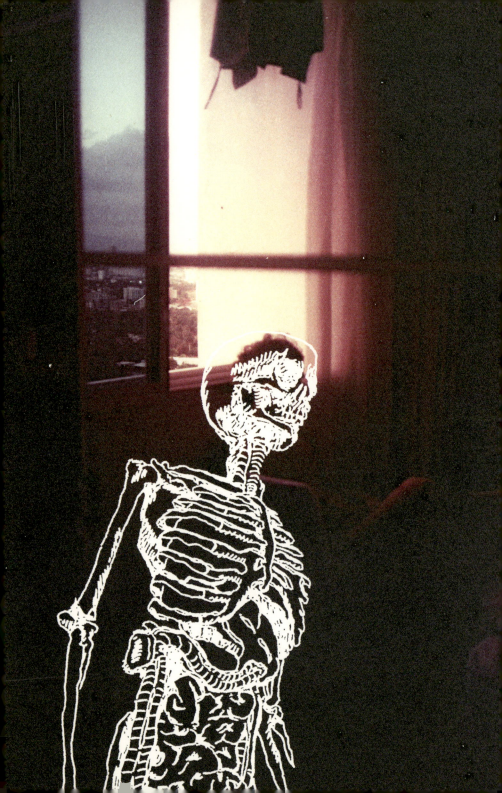

HALF-SPRUNG

The sun is asleep, but
my bones are warm;
laying awake past my bedtime
softly humming songs I learned
when I was
small.

There's a buzzing
static in my head,
too many thoughts
at once - I almost forgot
I am half
rot.

MONDAY FORGETS ABOUT THE DREAMERS

Sunday comes and goes
and Monday throws a stone
at your bedroom window and
promises she might give you reason
but we are stuck dreaming
within dreams
between bedsheets and phone
screens and when we squint
through cracks in blinds or
wind-blown gaps in curtains

there are twice as many stars as usual. *

*pays homage to The Two-Headed Calf by Laura Gilpin.

iii. *for Nietzsche*

"You have always approached everything terrible trustfully. You have wanted to pet every monster."

— Friedrich Nietzsche, *Thus Spoke Zarathustra*

SUNDAY MORNING PSYCHOSIS

Sharing half-rotten raspberries stuffed on fingertips with backyard dirt jammed under fingernails, because we're not afraid to get sick; hell, we're not even afraid to die. We haven't washed our hands in weeks and we haven't washed our hair, either. Sunday morning psychosis, they call it, something to do with the solitude or something to do with the Ritalin, but we dare not seek answers out of fear we'll be right. Our mother worries when we don't answer her calls but she can't smell the burning. Nobody can smell the burning. We look young for our age but act as if we're ancient and if you listen carefully enough we might just tell you why. Your secrets are safe with us, child. We don't have anyone to tell.

9.09 PM

TODAY I ATE THREE PEACHES, DANCED IN FRONT OF THE MIRROR, AND ~~DANCED~~ READ SOME THOMAS DE QUINCY. I MIGHT DREAM TONIGHT. I MIGHT THROW UP. I MISS YOU. ─────

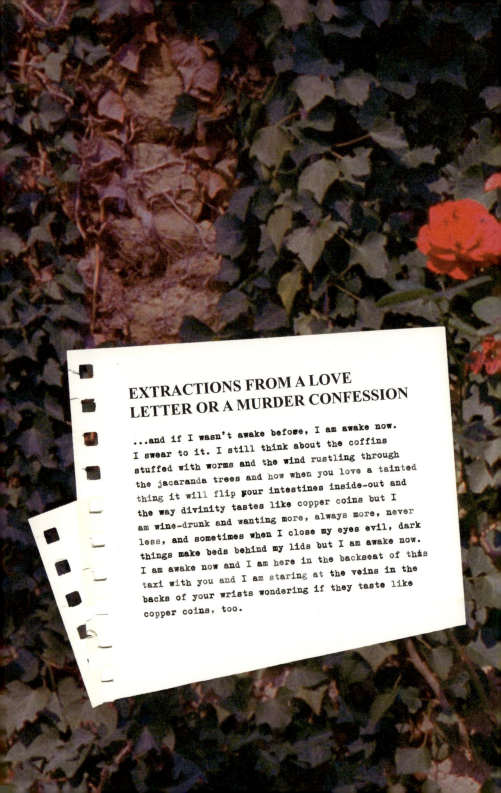

EXTRACTIONS FROM A LOVE LETTER OR A MURDER CONFESSION

...and if I wasn't awake before, I am awake now. I swear to it. I still think about the coffins stuffed with worms and the wind rustling through the jacaranda trees and how when you love a tainted thing it will flip your intestines inside-out and the way divinity tastes like copper coins but I am wine-drunk and wanting more, always more, never less, and sometimes when I close my eyes evil, dark things make beds behind my lids but I am awake now. I am awake now and I am here in the backseat of this taxi with you and I am staring at the veins in the backs of your wrists wondering if they taste like copper coins, too.

THE BLOOD ON HUMBERT'S HANDS

I could never really write love poems

I always liked them meaner,
               older,
                         boar-skinned and hellish

the kind with the ex-wives and the power
who preach purity like the pastor's son

the kind who blow murder into my lungs
condemning me to this perpetual youth.

(I wish this story ended

gently)

SUMMER'S SALVATION

In a place where blades of grass itch
at the skin of our bottle-cap ankles,
tucked beneath cracks in foliage
where light cascades in, soft and
dappled and rustling gardens too lush
to exist in our callous corner
of this darkened world -
it would be so easy, for you and me
to fake some kind of purity.
The air stinks of silver and if we stop
running and let it rest on our tongue,
we can almost taste
salvation.

SWITCHBLADE

I asked you why you kept a switchblade / in the back pocket of your baby blue jeans / when you left to go get milk and you shrugged / just in case / as you poured too much milk in my coffee. The coffee still burned my gums / and you still kissed me goodbye, only this time / a little longer. Was that just in case? You are black coffee / bitter lemons / toothpaste stains / cigarette kisses / and you are just in case. I am pinewood / chest pains / poisoned apples / dog-eared pages / and I am the switchblade / in the back pocket of your baby blue jeans / sharp and made for hunting.

PHILOSOPHY BETWEEN COTTON SHEETS

i. Your head is heavy on my chest. It makes me forget about the hollowness. It makes me forget my mother's maiden name before she was whole again, before the snakes had venom.

ii. We squint into the sun like it can give us an answer and let it burn our retinas because the doctors told us not to. Can you see it? you ask through gritted teeth. Can you see the space in between? I answer with thawing silence because we both know it's there. We've been living in it for three months now. We don't know how to get home.

iii. You can't count on me, I'm an absurdist. I tell you this from the start but your ears are filled with cornflakes and candle wax. You hear my first truth but you taste my last lie because I spit it with venom milked from the cobra in the plumbing pipes. The snakes are lethal now and they strike to kill and I know you're afraid but I can't take care of you here, not now, not like this, please, stop crying, please, learn how to take care of yourself. You can love an absurdist but she won't love you back. You can't see it. You stared too long at the sun.

THE SUN IS BOUND TO IMPLODE

The clouds
reflect in the river at dusk
and promise
absolution

      and I wonder:
if I take a step
into the centre will I drown
or be swallowed by
<u>heaven</u>

      and I wonder:
will the body found bloated
(almond eyes / fig-stained flesh)

or my dog with the amber eyes
rolling in reeds by the riverbank
wondering when I'll come home

be worth it.

ROT IN STAGES

I'll stick my fingers
                            down
                                            my throat

until you can stick your fingers
                                inside
                                            my rib cage

Until I'm
                rotten
                                instead
                                            of

        rotting.

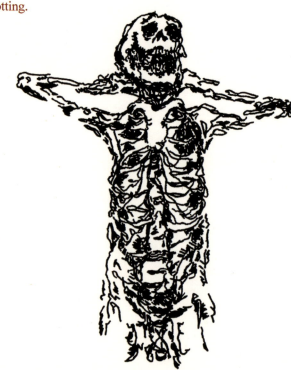

LILITH

I learned Hebrew in my dreams so
I could summon a deity in my wake.
Together we stain porcelain
veneers with bottom shelf merlot
and gossip about the goodness
left in the soil.
Earth eater,
secret keeper-
we walk a little too close to the sun
because we've come too far
for forgiveness.

INTRUSIVE THOUGHTS

I AM TRYING NOT TO THINK ABOUT:

black magic / is there a place for me in this world, or do I just exist? / why do I care so much? / setting things on fire / cake frosting / will I still write poetry once I am dead? / am I dead? / running away / throwing up / existential absurdism / decomposing under the shade of a wattle tree / you.

I AM TRYING NOT TO THINK ABOUT:

all of the lies I have told and forgotten / if I'm a good kisser / the tied up bodies in my neighbours garage / am I pretty? am I skinny? does this measure my worth? / climbing trees / the world ending / getting up for water between 3 and 4am / the voices I hear as I am falling asleep / you.

I AM TRYING NOT TO THINK ABOUT:

how many Hail Mary's I must speak to be saved / plucking out my eyelashes one by one / broken bones / the crows that leave gifts / do I want to fall in love? do I want someone to fall in love with me? / the words kept in Latin / summoning something sweet / sympathy for the cannibal / you / you / you.

I TRY. I TRY. I TRY.
I WRITE THE LISTS ANYWAY.

3:33 AM

WRITING BECOMES A DEMAND ONCE HUMAN BECOMES AUTHOR. THE NEAR FATAL RITE OF LANGUAGE TURNS ONE INTO A *HOMOS LUPUS*, LUSTFUL AND ACADEMIC AND ACHING FOR THE HUNT. WEREWOLF OR WRITER? WEREWOLVES ARE VICTIMS OF BLOODLUST BUT WRITERS ARE SLAVES TO IT. I WANT TO WRITE, BELIEVE ME, DEAR VOID; I YEARN TO WRITE, I BEG MYSELF TO BRING QUILL TO PARCHMENT. ALAS, THE METAPHYSICAL IS NOT SO SIMPLE. A GIRL CAN BE NO WOLF NOR GOD, YET SHE WILL NEVER STOP REACHING. DO YOU KNOW WHAT IT FEELS LIKE TO MISS SOMETHING YOU'VE NEVER HAD? DO YOU, DEAREST VOID? I DON'T BELIEVE IN MISTAKES ANY MORE BUT IF YOU HAD ASKED ME A YEAR AGO I WOULD'VE TOLD YOU THIS LIFE WAS ONE. THE GODS ARE IN HEAT AND IM NOT SURE I'M HUMAN AT ALL.

KLEOS

Achilles died at the hands of Apollo
but what good is a god to an agnostic?

We're all closeted deadbeats,
martyrs of whiskey and vomit
and unfinished poems.

Go home, little girl
this is no war.

(Achilles' weakness was pride,
not his heel.)

AN ODE TO THE AUSTRALIAN DIRT BENEATH MY FEET

The earth is parched but she is strong and she tells us this through cracks and slices in the fields of dirt stripped bare. It hasn't rained out here since the tooth fairy exchanged a golden coin for the last of my childhood. It was cavitied and loose and the dentist told me to yank extra hard or it would fill up with sugar and rot and die just like the cornfields. There's an air of archaic opulence, the precious filthy kind, and the horses canter on the dying earth as though she promised she wouldn't mind their hooves on her back. I don't know this yet, but I'll soon grow to hate the backyard snakes and the eucalyptus stench. But as the earth promised us she would live through the drought, I promise my teenage self I will grow to miss the gum-nut hail and maybe, just maybe, live to see her sprout.

85

87

ON SUN SWALLOWING

I dismantled my altar
in the heat of summer.
Lies can only last so long
before they rot your brain, so
perhaps my brain is stuffed with formaldehyde
or Stockholm syndrome
because I have not told a truth
for thirty-three days.

My mother doesn't know who I am anymore.
I think that should hurt
more than it does but
all I can taste is the sun in my throat, the sun
in my stomach, all effervescent and copper,
dappling my intestines in the lustre
of redemption.

I'll meet you
at the top
if I don't burn first.

CREDITS

poems	Dakota Warren
curation + direction	Abby Strangward Kyla Rain
editing	Ria Kealey
layout + design	Abby Strangward Dakota Warren
mixed-media collage	Kyla Rain
assistance	Levii Wishart
illustrations	Lydia Stone
photography	Caroline Dare Cheyenne Morschl-Villa Francesca McConnell Leche de Arte Clara Slewa Kyla Rain
printing	E-Plot Printing (special thanks to Karen Lawson)

Dakota Warren was born in rural Australia before running away to the city of Melbourne in her teen years. She is an avid reader, obsessive writer, and part-time god-killer. Her writings are an exploration of girlhood, godhood, nostalgia, hedonism, and the subtle yet excruciating enigma that is adulthood.

You can find her at dakotawarren.com or on Instagram at @fairy_bl00d